WHAT
DIFFERENCE
DOES PRAYER
MAKE?

WHAT DIFFERENCE DOES PRAYER MAKE?

PAUL E. MILLER

NAVPRESS

Discipleship Inside Out*

NAVPRESS
Discipleship Inside Out®

NavPress is the publishing ministry of The Navigators, an international Christian organization and leader in personal spiritual development. NavPress is committed to helping people grow spiritually and enjoy lives of meaning and hope through personal and group resources that are biblically rooted, culturally relevant, and highly practical.

For a free catalog go to www.NavPress.com
or call 1.800.366.7788 in the United States or 1.800.839.4769 in Canada.

"WHAT GOOD DOES IT DO?"

I was camping for the weekend in the Endless Mountains of Pennsylvania with five of our six kids. My wife, Jill, was home with our eight-year-old daughter, Kim. After a disastrous camping experience the summer before, Jill was happy to stay home. She said she was giving up camping for Lent.

I was walking down from our campsite to our Dodge Caravan when I noticed our fourteen-year-old daughter, Ashley, standing in front of the van, tense and upset. When I asked her what was wrong, she said, "I lost my contact lens. It's gone." I looked down with her at the forest floor, covered with leaves and twigs. There were a million little crevices for the lens to fall into and disappear.

I said, "Ashley, don't move. Let's pray." But before I could pray, she burst into tears.

"What good does it do? I've prayed for Kim to speak, and she isn't speaking."

Kim struggles with autism and developmental delay. Because of her weak fine motor skills and problems with motor planning, she is also mute. One day after five years of speech therapy, Kim crawled out of the speech therapist's office, crying from frustration. Jill said, "No more," and we stopped speech therapy.

Prayer was no mere formality for Ashley. She had taken God at his word and asked that he would let Kim speak. But nothing happened. Kim's muteness was testimony to a silent God. Prayer, it seemed, doesn't work.

Few of us have Ashley's courage to articulate the quiet cynicism or spiritual weariness that develops in us when heartfelt prayer goes unanswered. We keep our doubts hidden even from ourselves because we don't want to sound like bad Christians. No reason to add shame to our cynicism. So our hearts shut down.

The glib way people talk about prayer often reinforces our cynicism. We end our conversations with "I'll keep you in my prayers." We have a vocabulary of "prayer speak," including "I'll *lift you up* in prayer" and "I'll *remember* you in prayer." Many who use these phrases, including us, never get around to praying. Why? Because we don't think prayer makes much difference.

Cynicism and glibness are just part of the problem. The most common frustration is the activity of praying itself. We last for about fifteen seconds, and then out of nowhere the day's to-do list pops up and our minds are off on a tangent. We catch ourselves and, by sheer force of the will, go back to praying. Before we know it, it has happened again. Instead of praying, we are doing a confused mix of wandering and worrying. Then the guilt sets in. *Something must be wrong with me. Other Christians don't seem to have this trouble praying.* After five minutes we give up, saying, "I am no good at this. I might as well get some work done."

Something *is* wrong with us. Our natural desire to pray comes from Creation. We are made in the image of God. Our inability to pray comes from the Fall. Evil has marred the image. We want to talk to God but can't. The friction of our desire to pray, combined with our badly damaged prayer antennae, leads to constant frustration. It's as if we've had a stroke.

Complicating this is the enormous confusion about what makes for good prayer. We vaguely sense that we should begin by focusing on God, not on ourselves. So when we start to pray, we try to worship. That works for a minute, but it feels contrived; then guilt sets in again. We wonder, *Did I worship enough? Did I really mean it?*

In a burst of spiritual enthusiasm we put together a prayer list, but praying through the list gets dull, and nothing seems to happen. The list gets long and cumbersome; we lose touch with many of the needs. Praying feels like whistling in the wind. When someone is healed or helped, we wonder if it would have happened anyway. Then we misplace the list.

Praying exposes how self-preoccupied we are and uncovers our doubts. It was easier on our faith *not* to pray. After only a few minutes, our prayer is in shambles. Barely out of the starting gate, we collapse on the sidelines—cynical, guilty, and hopeless.

THE HARDEST PLACE IN THE WORLD TO PRAY

American culture is probably the hardest place in the world to learn to pray. We are so busy that when we slow down to pray, we find it uncomfortable. We prize accomplishments, production. But prayer is nothing but talking to God. It feels useless, as if we are wasting time. Every bone in our bodies screams, "Get to work."

When we aren't working, we are used to being entertained. Television, the Internet, video games, and cell phones make free time as busy as work. When we do slow down, we slip into a stupor. Exhausted by the pace of life, we veg out in front of a screen or with earplugs.

If we try to be quiet, we are assaulted by what C. S. Lewis called "the Kingdom of Noise."[1] Everywhere we go we hear background noise. If the noise isn't provided for us, we can bring our own via iPod.

Even our church services can have that same restless energy. There is little space to be still before God. We want our money's worth, so something should always be happening.

We are uncomfortable with silence.

One of the subtlest hindrances to prayer is probably the most pervasive. In the broader culture and in our churches, we prize intellect, competency, and wealth. Because we can do life without God, praying seems nice but unnecessary. Money can do what prayer does, and it is quicker and less time-consuming. Our trust in ourselves and in our talents makes us structurally independent of God. As a result, exhortations to pray don't stick.

THE ODDNESS OF PRAYING

It's worse if we stop and think about how odd prayer is. When we have a phone conversation, we hear a voice and can respond. When we pray, we are talking to air. Only crazy people talk to themselves. How do we talk with a Spirit, with someone who doesn't speak with an audible voice?

And if we believe that God can talk to us in prayer, how do we distinguish our thoughts from his thoughts? Prayer is confusing. We vaguely know that the Holy Spirit is somehow involved, but we are never sure how or when a spirit will show up or what that even means. Some people seem to have a lot of the Spirit. We don't.

Forget about God for a minute. Where do you fit in? Can you pray for what you want? And what's the point of praying if God already knows what you need? Why bore God? It sounds like nagging. Just thinking about prayer ties us all up in knots.

Has this been your experience? If so, know that you have lots of company. Most Christians feel frustrated when it comes to prayer!

A VISIT TO A PRAYER THERAPIST

Let's imagine that you see a prayer therapist to get your prayer life straightened out. The therapist says, "Let's begin by looking at your relationship with your heavenly Father. God said, 'I will be a father to you, and you shall be sons and daughters to me' (2 Corinthians 6:18). What does it mean that you are a son or daughter of God?"

You reply that it means you have complete

access to your heavenly Father through Jesus. You have true intimacy, based not on how good you are but on the goodness of Jesus. Not only that, Jesus is your brother. You are a fellow heir with him.

The therapist smiles and says, "That is right. You've done a wonderful job of describing the *doctrine* of Sonship. Now tell me what it is like for you to *be with* your Father? What is it like to *talk* with him?"

You cautiously tell the therapist how difficult it is to be in your Father's presence, even for a couple of minutes. Your mind wanders. You aren't sure what to say. You wonder, *Does prayer make any difference? Is God even there?* Then you feel guilty for your doubts and just give up.

Your therapist tells you what you already suspect. "Your relationship with your heavenly Father is dysfunctional. You talk as if you have an intimate relationship, but you don't. Theoretically, it is close. Practically, it is distant. You need help."

ASHLEY'S CONTACT

I needed help when Ashley burst into tears in front of our minivan. I was frozen, caught between her doubts and my own. I had no idea that she'd been praying for Kim to speak. What made Ashley's tears so disturbing was that she was right. God had not answered her prayers. Kim was still mute. I was fearful for my daughter's faith and for my own. I did not know what to do.

Would I make the problem worse by praying? If we prayed and couldn't find the contact, it would just confirm Ashley's growing unbelief. Already, Jill and I were beginning to lose her heart. Her childhood faith in God was being replaced by faith in boys. Ashley was cute, warm, and outgoing. Jill was having trouble keeping track of Ashley's boyfriends, so she started naming them like ancient kings. Ashley's first boyfriend was Frank, so his successors became Frank the Second, Frank the Third, and so on. Jill and I needed help.

I had little confidence God would do anything, but I prayed silently, *Father, this would be a really good time to come through. You've got to hear this prayer for the sake of*

Ashley. Then I prayed aloud with Ashley, *Father, help us to find this contact.*

When I finished, we bent down to look through the dirt and twigs. There, sitting on a leaf, was the missing lens.

Prayer made a difference after all.

BECOME LIKE A LITTLE CHILD

On more than one occasion, Jesus tells his disciples to become like little children. The most famous is when the young mothers try to get near Jesus so he can bless their infants. When the disciples block them, Jesus rebukes his disciples sharply. "Let the children come to me; do not hinder them, for to such belongs the kingdom of God. Truly, I say to you, whoever does not receive the kingdom of God like a child shall not enter it" (Mark 10:14-15). Jesus' rebuke would have surprised the disciples. It would have seemed odd. Children in the first century weren't considered cute or innocent. Only since the nineteenth-century Romantic era have we idolized children.[2]

Another incident occurs when the

disciples are traveling and begin arguing with one another as to who is the greatest (see Mark 9:33-37). When they get to Peter's house in Capernaum, Jesus asks them what they were talking about on the way. The disciples just look at the ground and shuffle their feet. At first Jesus says nothing. He sits down, takes a little boy, and has him stand in their midst. Then Jesus picks him up and, while holding him, says, "Unless you turn and become like children, you will never enter the kingdom of heaven" (Matthew 18:3). Little children, even in adult form, are important to Jesus.

Jesus wants us to be without pretense when we come to him in prayer. Instead, we often try to be something we aren't. We begin by concentrating on God, but almost immediately our minds wander off in a dozen different directions. The problems of the day push out our well-intentioned resolve to be spiritual. We give ourselves a spiritual kick in the pants and try again, but life crowds out prayer. We know that prayer isn't supposed to be like this, so we give up in despair. We might as well get something done.

What's the problem? We're trying to be

spiritual, to get it right. We know we don't need to clean up our act in order to become a Christian, but when it comes to praying, we forget that. We, like adults, try to fix ourselves up. In contrast, Jesus wants us to come to him like little children, just as we are.

COME MESSY

The difficulty of coming just as we are is that we are messy. And prayer makes it worse. When we slow down to pray, we are immediately confronted with how unspiritual we are, with how difficult it is to concentrate on God. We didn't know how bad we were until we tried to be good. Nothing exposes our selfishness and spiritual powerlessness like prayer.

In contrast, little children never get frozen by their selfishness. Like the disciples, they come just as they are, totally self-absorbed. They seldom get it right. As parents or friends, we know all that. In fact, we are delighted (most of the time!) to find out what is on their little hearts. We don't scold them for being self-absorbed or fearful. That is just who they are.

This isn't just a random observation about how parents respond to little children. This is the gospel, the welcoming heart of God. God also cheers when we come to him with our wobbling, unsteady prayers. Jesus does not say, "Come to me, all you who have learned how to concentrate in prayer, whose minds no longer wander, and I will give you rest." No, Jesus opens his arms to his needy children and says, "Come to Me, all who are weary and heavy-laden, and I will give you rest" (Matthew 11:28, NASB). The criteria for coming to Jesus is weariness. Come overwhelmed with life. Come with your wandering mind. Come messy.

What does it feel like to be weary? You have trouble concentrating. The problems of the day are like claws in your brain. You feel pummeled by life.

What does heavy-laden feel like? Same thing. You have so many problems you don't even know where to start. You can't do life on your own anymore. Jesus wants you to come to him that way! Your weariness drives you to him.

Don't try to get the prayer right; just tell

God where you are and what's on your mind. That's what little children do. They come as they are, runny noses and all. Like the disciples, they just say what is on their minds.

We know that to become a Christian we shouldn't try to fix ourselves up, but when it comes to praying we completely forget that. We'll sing the old gospel hymn "Just as I Am," but when it comes to praying, we don't come just as we are. We try, like adults, to fix ourselves up.

Private, personal prayer is one of the last great bastions of legalism. In order to pray like a child, you might need to unlearn the nonpersonal, nonreal praying that you've been taught.

THE REAL YOU

Why is it so important to come to God just as you are? If you don't, then you are artificial and unreal, like the Pharisees. Rarely did they tell Jesus directly what they were thinking. Jesus accused them of being hypocrites, of being masked actors with two faces. They weren't real. Nor did they like little children.

The Pharisees were indignant when the little children poured into the temple (after Jesus had cleansed it) and began worshipping him. Jesus replied, quoting Psalm 8, "Out of the mouth of infants and nursing babies you have prepared praise" (Matthew 21:16).

The only way to come to God is by taking off any spiritual mask. The real you has to meet the real God. He is a person.

So, instead of being frozen by your self-preoccupation, talk with God about your worries. Tell him where you are weary. If you don't begin with where you are, then where you are will sneak in the back door. Your mind will wander to where you are weary.

We are often so busy and overwhelmed that when we slow down to pray, we don't know where our hearts are. We don't know what troubles us. So, oddly enough, we might have to worry before we pray. Then our prayers will make sense. They will be about our real lives.

Your heart could be, and often is, askew. That's okay. You have to begin with what is real. Jesus didn't come for the righteous. He came for sinners. All of us qualify. The very things we try to get rid of—our weariness, our distractedness, our messiness—are what get us in the front door! That's how the gospel works. That's how prayer works.

In bringing your real self to Jesus, you give him the opportunity to work on the real you, and you will slowly change. The kingdom will come. You'll end up less selfish.

The kingdom comes when Jesus becomes king of your life. But it has to be *your life*. You can't create a kingdom that doesn't exist, where you try to be better than you really are. Jesus calls that hypocrisy—putting on a mask to cover the real you.

Ironically, many attempts to teach people to pray encourage the creation of a split personality. You're taught to "do it right." Instead of the real, messy you meeting God, you try to re-create yourself by becoming spiritual.

No wonder prayer is so unsatisfying.

So instead of being paralyzed by who you are, begin with who you are. That's how the gospel works. God begins with you. It's a little scary because you are messed up.

TOUCHING OUR FATHER'S HEART

The opening words of the Lord's Prayer are *Our Father*. You are the center of your heavenly Father's affection. That is where you find rest for your soul. If you remove prayer from the welcoming heart of God (as much teaching on the Lord's Prayer does), prayer becomes a legalistic chore. We do the duty but miss touching the heart of God. By coming to God "weary and heavy-laden," we discover his heart; heaven touches earth and his will is done.

We have much more to learn about praying, but by coming like a little child to our Father, we have learned the heart of prayer. I say "we" deliberately because I regularly forget the simplicity of prayer. I become depressed, and after failing to fix my depression, I give up on myself and remain distant from God. I forget the openness of my Father's heart. He wants me to come depressed, just as I am.

ASKING LIKE A CHILD

Let's do a quick analysis on how little children ask.

What do they ask for? Everything and anything. If they hear about Disneyland, they want to go there tomorrow.

How often do little children ask? Repeatedly. Over and over again. They wear us out. Sometimes we give in just to shut them up.

How do little children ask? Without guile. They just say what is on their minds. They have no awareness of what is appropriate or inappropriate.

Jesus tells us to watch little children if we want to learn how to ask in prayer. After introducing the idea of bold asking in the Sermon on the Mount ("Ask, and it will be given to you"), he tells us why we can boldly ask. "Which one of you, if his son asks him for bread, will give him a stone? Or if he asks for a fish, will give him a serpent? If you then, who are evil, know how to give good gifts to your children, how much more will your Father who is in heaven give good things to those who ask him!" (Matthew 7:7,9-11).

When our son John was six months old, he stuck out his hand in the general direction of the butter and said "bubu." We didn't say, "John, you should say 'please.' And it's not 'bubu,' but B-U-T-T-E-R. Furthermore, there is a self-orientation here that if left unchecked will ruin your life." *Bubu* was our son's first word, so we laughed and gave him the butter.

Kim got her first speech computer when she was five years old. We took it down to the Jersey shore for vacation. We explained the keys to her and waited. She leaned over and pressed the key with little McDonald's golden arches on it. The electronic voice came to life and said "McDonald's." It was two o'clock in the afternoon, and we'd just eaten lunch. We dropped everything, leapt into the car with Kim, raced off to McDonald's, and got Kim a hamburger and a soda. We were thrilled. It wasn't long before she was ordering her entire meal at McDonald's. She's particularly happy if Mom isn't around so she can get french fries.

If we earthly parents, with all our broken-ness, still give our kids good gifts, won't our heavenly Father do even more? Our kids' requests, no matter how trivial, tug at our hearts. God feels the same.

BELIEVING LIKE A CHILD

The next thing we must do in learning to pray is believe like a child. Children are supremely confident of their parents' love and power. Instinctively, they trust. They believe their parents want to do them good. If you know your parent loves and protects you, it fills your world with possibility. You just chatter away with what is on your heart.

It works the same in the world of prayer. If you learn to pray, you learn to dream again. I say "again" because every child naturally dreams and hopes. To learn how to pray is to enter the world of a child, where all things are possible. Little children can't imagine that their parents won't eventually say yes. They know if they keep pestering their parents, they'll eventually give in. Childlike faith drives this persistence.

But as we get older, we get less naïve and more cynical. Disappointment and broken promises are the norm instead of hoping and dreaming. Our childlike faith dies a thousand little deaths. Jesus encourages us to believe like little children by telling stories about adults who acted like children: the parable of the persistent widow, who won't take no for an answer from an unjust judge (see Luke 18:1-8), and the parable about a man who badgers his neighbor to lend him three loaves for a friend who has come at midnight (see Luke 11:5-8).

On the rare occasion when Jesus encounters an adult who believes like a child, he stands on a soapbox and practically yells, "Pay attention to this person. Look how he or she believes!" He only does that twice; both times the person was a Gentile, from outside of the community of faith. The first is a Roman officer, a centurion, who is so confident of Jesus' ability to heal his paralyzed servant that he asks Jesus to heal without even visiting his home. He tells Jesus, "But say the word, and let my servant be healed" (Luke 7:7). Jesus is stunned. He turns to the crowd following him and says, "I tell you, not even in Israel have I found such faith" (7:9). The second is a Canaanite woman whose daughter is possessed by a demon. Even though Jesus rebuffs her, she keeps coming back. Jesus marvels at her faith, giving her his second Great Faith Oscar: "Woman, great is your faith! Be it done for you as you desire" (Matthew 15:28).

Earlier we saw that believing the gospel—knowing God's acceptance for us in Jesus—helps us to come to him messy. Now we see that the gospel also frees us to ask for what is on our hearts.

LEARNING TO PLAY AGAIN

Besides asking and believing like a child, learning to pray involves, surprisingly, learning to play again. How do little children play? If you ask a parent how long a one-year-old stays on task, he or she just smiles. But if you must know, it varies anywhere from three seconds to three minutes. It isn't long, nor is it particularly organized.

How can that teach us to pray? Think for a minute. How do we structure our adult conversations? We don't. Especially when talking with old friends, the conversation bounces from subject to subject. It has a fun, meandering, play-like quality. Why would our prayer time be any different? After all, God is a person.

Prayer that lacks this play-like quality is almost autistic. When you are autistic, you have trouble picking up social clues from the other person. For instance, Kim calls me around one thirty when she gets home from work. She presses the speaker button on our phone, dials my cell, and tells me on her speech computer how her day went. She never says "hi"; she just jumps into a description of her day and hangs up. No questions. No "good-bye" or "see you later." Just click.

When your mind starts wandering in prayer, be like a little child. Don't worry about being organized or staying on task. Remember you are in conversation with a person. Instead of beating yourself up, learn to play again. Pray about what your mind is wandering to. Maybe it is something that is important to you. Maybe the Spirit is nudging you to think about something else.

UNDERSTANDING CYNICISM

The opposite of a childlike spirit is a cynical spirit. Cynicism is, increasingly, the dominant spirit of our age. Personally, it is my greatest struggle in prayer. If I get an answer to prayer, sometimes I'll think, *It would have happened anyway.* Other times I'll try to pray but wonder if it makes any difference.

Many Christians stand at the edge of cynicism, struggling with a defeated weariness. Their spirits have begun to deaden, but unlike the cynic, they've not lost hope. My friend Bryan summarized it this way: "I think we have built up scar tissue from our frustrations, and we don't want to expose ourselves anymore. Fear constrains us."

Cynicism and defeated weariness have this in common: They both question the active goodness of God on our behalf. Left unchallenged, their low-level doubt opens the door for bigger doubt. They've lost their childlike spirit and thus are unable to move toward their heavenly Father.

When I say that cynicism is the spirit of the age, I mean it is an influence, a tone that permeates our culture, one of the master temptations of our age. By reflecting on cynicism and defeated weariness, we are meditating on the last petition of the Lord's Prayer: "Lead us not into temptation, but deliver us from the evil one" (Matthew 6:13, NIV).

Cynicism is so pervasive that, at times, it feels like a presence. Behind the spirit of the age lies an unseen, personal evil presence, a spirit. If Satan can't stop you from praying, then he will try to rob the fruit of praying by dulling your soul. Satan cannot create, but he can corrupt.

THE FEEL OF CYNICISM

Satan's first recorded words are cynical. He tells Adam and Eve, "For God knows that when you eat of it your eyes will be opened, and you will be like God" (Genesis 3:5). Satan is suggesting that God's motives are cynical. In essence, he tells them, "God has not been honest about the tree in the middle of the garden. The command not to eat from the tree isn't for your protection; God wants to protect himself from rivals. He's jealous. He is projecting an image of caring for you, but he really has an agenda to protect himself. God has two faces." Satan seductively gives Adam and Eve the inside track—here is what is *really* going on behind closed doors. Such is the deadly intimacy that gossip offers.

Satan sees evil everywhere, even in God himself. Ironically, it became a self-fulfilling prophecy. Since the Fall, evil feels omnipresent, making cynicism an easy sell. Because cynicism sees what is "really going on," it feels real, authentic. That gives cynicism an elite status since authenticity is one of the last remaining public virtues in our culture.

To be cynical is to be distant. While offering a false intimacy of being "in the know," cynicism actually destroys intimacy. It leads to a creeping bitterness that can deaden and even destroy the spirit.

A praying life is just the opposite. It engages evil. It doesn't take no for an answer. The psalmist was in God's face, hoping, dreaming, asking. Prayer is feisty. Cynicism, on the other hand, merely critiques. It is passive, cocooning itself off from the passions of the great cosmic battle we are engaged in. It is without hope.

If you add an overlay of prayer to a cynical or even weary heart, it feels phony. For the cynic, life is already phony; you feel as if you are just contributing to the mess.

A JOURNEY INTO CYNICISM

Cynicism begins, oddly enough, with too much of the wrong kind of faith, with *naïve optimism* or foolish confidence. At first glance, genuine faith and naïve optimism appear identical since both foster confidence and hope. But the similarity is only surface deep. Genuine faith comes from knowing my heavenly Father loves, enjoys, and cares for me. Naïve optimism is groundless. It is childlike trust without the loving Father.

The movement from naïve optimism to cynicism is the new American journey. In naïve optimism we don't need to pray because everything is under control, everything is possible. In cynicism we can't pray because everything is out of control, little is possible.

With the Good Shepherd no longer leading us through the valley of the shadow of death, we need something to maintain our sanity. Cynicism's ironic stance is a weak attempt to maintain a lighthearted equilibrium in a world gone mad. These aren't just benign cultural trends; they are your life.

At some point, each of us comes face-to-face with the valley of the shadow of death. We can't ignore it. We can't remain neutral with evil. We either give up and distance ourselves, or we learn to walk with the Shepherd. There is no middle ground.

Without the Good Shepherd, we are alone in a meaningless story. Weariness and fear leave us feeling overwhelmed, unable to move. Cynicism leaves us doubting, unable to dream. The combination shuts down our hearts, and we just show up for life, going through the motions. Some days it's difficult to get out of our pajamas.

Our personal struggles with cynicism and defeated weariness are reinforced by an increasing tendency toward perfectionism in American culture. Believing you have to have the perfect relationship, the perfect children, or a perfect body sets you up for a critical spirit, the breeding ground for cynicism. In the absence of perfection, we resort to spin—trying to make ourselves look good, unwittingly dividing ourselves into a public and private self. We cease to be real and become the subject of cynicism.

FOLLOWING JESUS OUT OF CYNICISM

Jesus offers six cures for cynicism. Let's look at them in turn.

1. Be Warm but Wary

Jesus does not ignore evil. When he sends the disciples on their first missionary journey, he says, "I am sending you out as sheep in the midst of wolves, so be wise as serpents and innocent as doves" (Matthew 10:16). The overwhelming temptation when faced with evil is to become a wolf, to become cynical and lose your sheeplike spirit. Jesus tells us to instead be warm but wary—warm like a dove but wary like a serpent.

Jesus keeps in tension wariness about evil with a robust confidence in the goodness of his Father. He continues, "Beware of men" (10:17); then in the next breath he warms our hearts to our Father's love, saying, "Fear not, therefore; you are of more value than many sparrows" (10:31). Since your Father is intimately involved with the death of even one sparrow, won't he watch over your life? You don't have to distance yourself with an ironic, critical stance. You don't have to shut down your heart in the face of evil. You can engage it.

Instead of naïve optimism, Jesus calls us to be wary, yet confident in our heavenly Father. We are to combine a robust trust in the Good Shepherd with a vigilance about the presence of evil in our own hearts and in the hearts of others.

The feel of a praying life is cautious optimism—caution because of the Fall, optimism because of redemption. Cautious optimism allows Jesus to boldly send his disciples into an evil world.

Our confidence in the face of evil comes directly from the spirit of Jesus and animates a praying spirit. Audacious faith is one of the hallmarks of Jesus' followers. As we shall see later, praying is the principal way we enter into this expansion of the rule of Christ.

Jesus isn't just offering practical wisdom. His wisdom works because in his death he himself acted boldly, trusting his Father to help him. While Jesus is hanging on the cross, the religious leaders cynically mock him for his childlike trust. "He saved others; he cannot save himself. . . . He trusts in God; let God deliver him" (Matthew 27:42-43). In effect they are saying, "Look what happens when you act like a child and trust your Father. He abandons you." They accuse Jesus of naïveté, of acting foolishly because he believes in God's goodness.

Jesus does not answer his mockers because his ear is tuned to his Father. Like a wise serpent, he says nothing. Like a harmless dove, he does nothing. Even as his Father turns his back on him, Jesus trusts. Faced with the storm of life, he tightens his grip on his Father.

Jesus' childlike faith delighted his Father, and on Easter morning his Father acted on Jesus' dead body, bringing him to life. *He trusted in God; God delivered him.* Evil did not have the last word. Hope was born.

2. Learn to Hope Again

Cynicism kills hope. The world of the cynic is fixed and immovable; the cynic believes we are swept along by forces greater than we are. Dreaming feels like so much foolishness. Risk becomes intolerable. Prayer feels pointless, as if we are talking to the wind. Why set ourselves and God up for failure?

But Jesus is all about hope. Watch what he says *before* he helps these people. Before he heals a blind man, he tells his disciples that "this happened so that the work of God might be displayed in his life" (John 9:3, NIV). Before he raises the widow of Nain's son, he tells her, "Weep not" (Luke 7:13, KJV), reversing the ancient Jewish funeral dirge, "Weep, all that are bitter of heart." When Jairus tells Jesus that his daughter is dead, Jesus says, "Do not fear; only believe" (Luke 8:50). Before Jesus heals a crippled woman, he tells her, "Woman, you are freed from your disability" (Luke 13:12). In each of these accounts, Jesus brings hope before he heals. He is not a healing machine—he touches people's hearts, healing their souls before he heals their bodies.

Hope begins with the heart of God. As you grasp what the Father's heart is like, how he loves to give, then prayer will begin to feel completely natural to you.

Many of us believe in the Christian hope of ultimate redemption, but we breathe the cynical spirit of our age and miss the heart of God. This was brought home to me when I discovered from a widow that her husband's philosophy of life went like this: "Expect nothing. Then if something good happens, be thankful." He had been a dear friend and godly counselor to me, but I was so surprised that I blurted out to his wife a confused mix of Romans 15:13 and Hebrews 13:20—"Sue, that sounds so different from 'May the God of hope, who brought again from the dead our Lord Jesus, fill you with all joy and peace in believing, so that by the power of the Holy Spirit you may abound in hope.'" Paul and the writer of Hebrews were bursting with the goodness of God. It spilled out of their hearts.

3. Cultivate a Childlike Spirit

I recently had a cynical moment during my morning prayer time. I was reflecting on some answers to the previous day's prayer, and I felt a lingering distaste in my soul. All I'd done was pray, and God had acted. It seemed too easy. Trite. I realized I was hunting for something to doubt. I was also hunting for something to do. At bottom, I didn't like grace. I wanted to be a player in the way God answered my request. In fact, at that moment I didn't like God. I was more comfortable with his distance.

What do I do with this old heart of mine? Exactly what we have been talking about. Cry out for grace like a hungry child. As soon as I begin simply asking for help, I have become like a little child again. I've stopped becoming cynical. Oddly enough, my prayer is answered almost immediately because in the act of praying I've become like a child. The cure for cynicism is to become like a little child again. Instead of critiquing others' stories, watch the story our Father is weaving.

Years ago I went through a time when my life became so difficult I was unable to pray. I couldn't concentrate. So I stopped trying to have a coherent prayer time, and for weeks on end during my morning prayer time, I did nothing but pray through Psalm 23. I was fighting for my life. I didn't realize it at the time, but I was following the habit of divine reading, called *lectio divina*, which was developed by the early church. By praying slowly through a portion of Scripture, I was allowing Scripture to shape my prayers.

As I prayed through Psalm 23, I began to reflect on the previous day and to look for the Shepherd's presence, for his touches of love. Even on especially hard days, I began to notice him everywhere, setting a table before me in the presence of my enemies, pursuing me with his love. Both the child and the cynic walk through the valley of the shadow of death. The cynic focuses on the darkness; the child focuses on the Shepherd.

The Shepherd's presence in the dark valley is so immediate, so powerful, that cynicism simply vanishes. There is no room for an ironic disengagement when you are fighting for your life. As you cling to the Shepherd, the fog of cynicism lifts.

Because cynicism misses the presence of the Shepherd, it reverses the picture in John 1 of light invading darkness. Like Saruman in

The Lord of the Rings, cynicism looks too long into the Dark Lord's crystal ball. Its attempt to unmask evil unwittingly enlarges evil. Increasingly, we are returning to the world of pre-Christian paganism, where evil seemingly has the loudest voice and the last word.

A childlike spirit interprets life through the lens of Psalm 23. Jesus acts out Psalm 23 at the feeding of the five thousand. When he sees that the crowds are "like sheep without a shepherd," he feeds them spiritually by "teach[ing] them many things." Then he has them "sit down . . . on the green grass" and feeds them with so much food that their baskets overflow (Mark 6:34-44).

Jesus meditates on Psalm 22 to prepare for his death. On the cross, overwhelmed by evil, he recites Psalm 22:1: "My God, my God, why have you forsaken me?" In the darkness, Jesus doesn't analyze what he doesn't know. He clings to what he knows.

4. Cultivate a Thankful Spirit

Immersing myself in Psalm 23 became a habit during this period of suffering. Prayer wasn't self-discipline; it was desperation. I began by thanking God for his touches of grace from the previous day. Either I thanked God or I gave into bitterness, the stepchild of cynicism. There was no middle ground.

Now years later, I still begin my prayer times by reflecting on the Shepherd's care. I drift through the previous day and watch God at work. Nothing undercuts cynicism more than a spirit of thankfulness. You begin to realize that your whole life is a gift.

Thankfulness isn't a matter of forcing yourself to see the happy side of life. That would be like returning to naïve optimism. Thanking God restores the natural order of our dependence on God. It enables us to see life as it really is.

Not surprisingly, thanklessness is the first sin to emerge from our ancient rebellion against God. Paul wrote, "For although they knew God, they did not honor him as God or give thanks to him" (Romans 1:21).

Paul's own life reflects a spirit of thanksgiving. Almost every time he described how he prayed for people, he mentioned thanksgiving. To become thankful is to be drawn into the fellowship of the Father, the Son, and the Spirit, into their enjoyment of one another, of life, and of people.

Cynicism looks reality in the face, calls it phony, and prides itself on its insight as it pulls back. Thanksgiving looks reality in the face and rejoices at God's care. It replaces a bitter spirit with a generous one.

In the face of Adam and Eve's evil, God takes up needle and thread and patiently sews fine leather clothing for them (see Genesis 3:21). He covers their divided, hiding selves with love. The same God permits his Son to be stripped naked so we could be clothed. God is not cynical in the face of evil. He loves.

5. Practice Repentance

Cynics imagine they are disinterested observers on a quest for authenticity. They assume they are humble because they offer nothing. In fact, they feel deeply superior because they think they see through everything.

C. S. Lewis pointed out that if you see through everything, you eventually see nothing.

You cannot go on "explaining away" for ever: you will find that you have explained explanation itself away. You cannot go on "seeing through" things for ever. The whole point of seeing through something is to see something through it. . . . If you see through everything, then everything is transparent. But a wholly transparent world is an invisible world. To "see through" all things is the same as not to see.[3]

Lewis said that what was required was a restoration of the innocent eye, the eye that can see with wonder.[4] That is the eye of a child.

While purporting to "see through" others' façades, cynics lack purity of heart. A significant source of cynicism is the fracture between my heart and my behavior. It goes something like this: My heart gets out of tune with God, but life goes on. So I continue to perform and say Christian things, but they are just words. I talk about Jesus without the presence of Jesus. There is a disconnect between what I present and who I am. My words sound phony, so others' words sound phony too. In short, my empty religious performance leads me to think that everyone is phony. The very thing I am doing, I accuse others of doing. Adding judgment to hypocrisy breeds cynicism.

All sin involves a splitting of the personality—what James calls being "double-minded" (4:8). If we become proud, we have an inflated sense of self that has lost touch with who we really are. If a husband watches porn online and then warmly greets his wife, he has created two people—one public and one hidden. If you talk about friends disparagingly behind their backs, you've created two personalities—the loving friend and the gossiping friend. You try to keep the personalities separate by telling those to whom you gossip, "Please keep this in confidence."

We first see this split immediately after Adam and Eve sin. Their friendly, walking-with-God selves are replaced by hiding, naked selves. God's searching question, "Where are you?" (Genesis 3:9), attempts to expose this fracture of the two selves.

Repentance brings the split personality

together and thus restores integrity to the life. The real self is made public. When the proud person is humbled, the elevated self is united with the true self.

In contrast, cynicism focuses on the other person's split personality and need to repent. It lacks the humility that comes from first taking the beam out of its own eye. Jesus says, "You hypocrite, first take the log out of your own eye, and then you will see clearly to take the speck out of your brother's eye" (Matthew 7:5).

You see these dynamics when David arrives at King Saul's camp, bringing food for his older brothers. David is surprised to hear Goliath taunting the Israelites and their God. He is shocked that no one has the courage to challenge Goliath and blurts out, "Who is this uncircumcised Philistine, that he should defy the armies of the living God?" (1 Samuel 17:26). David reacts to the split between Israel's public faith and its battlefield cowardice.

David has been off by himself, separated from the current of unbelief dominating his culture, developing a rich walk with the

Shepherd. David's obscurity has protected him from the cynical spirit of the age. His public faith and private practice are in harmony. His *normal* is experiencing God's presence in the valley of the shadow of death, where he has killed both lions and bears with his sling. Goliath just looks like a big bear. The result? Israel's unbelief feels odd, out of place.

When David's older brother Eliab gets wind of David questioning the other soldiers, he mocks David: "Why have you come down? And with whom have you left those few sheep in the wilderness? I know your presumption and the evil of your heart, for you have come down to see the battle" (17:28). Eliab mistakenly believes he sees right through his brother's motivations. He thinks that David, bored with the sheep, is there for adventure, egging the soldiers on so he can see a battle. Eliab's perception of David's motivation is likely his own motivation. He reads his own issues into David, cynically accusing his little brother of having cynical motives. Eliab lacks purity of heart, so he presumes David lacks it as well.

We see the same dynamics in the Garden

of Eden. Satan accuses God of cynical motivations, when in fact Satan cynically twists God's commands to his own ends. Cynicism is the seed for Adam and Eve's rebellion against God, and it is the seed for our own personal rebellions. While attempting to unmask evil, the cynic creates it.

Eliab also sees himself incorrectly. He has a false, elevated view of himself. He mocks David's lowly job as a shepherd: "With whom have you left those few sheep in the wilderness?" Eliab the Mighty Warrior mocks his little brother's sheep tending while the real Eliab is cowering in his tent with the rest of the Israelites.

David brushes aside Eliab's cynicism and ends up with Saul's blessing and armor. He quickly realizes that he can't fight in Saul's armor. He can't be something he is not. He is a shepherd, not a warrior. His inner and outer lives need to match. He is authentic.

David reaches for his staff, gathers five smooth stones from the creek, and moves toward Goliath. Goliath, enraged by the insult of the Israelites sending only a boy, misses the sling and sees only the staff. "Am I a dog, that you come to me with sticks?" (17:43).

David's reply evokes the spirit of prayer: "The LORD saves not with sword and spear. For the battle is the LORD's, and he will give you into our hand" (17:47). David quickens his pace. The closer he is, the greater the stone's velocity and the more accurate the placement. Goliath never even sees it coming.

Like David, the pure in heart begin with seeing through themselves. Having confronted their own bears and lions in the valley of the shadow of death, they see clearly the abnormality of Goliath cursing the living God. By cultivating a lifestyle of repentance, the pure in heart develop integrity, and their own fractures are healed. By beginning with their own impurity, they avoid the critical, negative stance of cynicism.

The good news is that by following Jesus we don't have to be captured by the spirit of the age. We don't have to be defined by our culture. Like Paul in Philippi, we can sing in jail (see Acts 16:25). Like David, we can calmly pick up five smooth stones when faced with overwhelming odds.

6. Develop an Eye for Jesus

Jill and I manage a part-time, seasonal tax business on the side. Several years ago I arrived at the office at eight in the morning for a quick visit before customers arrived. I was depressed, struggling with cynicism and even bouts of unbelief. I noticed the computer's hard drive was almost full, so I decided to delete an old program. Without thinking, I clicked "yes" to "Delete all shared files?" and I got the blue screen of death. The computer was dead.

I glanced at the appointment book and saw our first appointment wasn't due until eleven thirty. The next several hours were a frenzy of activity, calling help desks and hunting for backup disks. But the problem still wasn't fixed when our customer walked in. I asked our preparer to tell her that we'd be ready "any minute now."

I needed to go home to get a disk, so I slunk past our "eleven thirty," avoiding eye contact. It was close to noon when I slipped by her again to get a backup computer. I stole a glance at her and noticed that she was sitting quietly, without a hint of impatience. When I came back at one, she was still waiting serenely. Her calm demeanor was unchanged when we finally did her tax return at three o'clock.

I am not kidding—this woman sat in our office for three and a half hours without a single question or complaint. And this is Philadelphia! She'd taken the bus, so I offered to drive her home. Depressed and frustrated, I blurted out, "Does Jesus make a difference in your life?" (I thought she might be Catholic.) Please understand, I was not witnessing—I wanted to be witnessed to. She replied, "Jesus is everything to me. I talk to him all the time."

I was floored, partly by the freshness and simplicity of her faith but mainly by the unusual patience that displayed her faith. My frantic busyness was a sharp contrast to her quiet waiting in prayer. She reflected the spirit of prayer. I reflected the spirit of human self-sufficiency.

I'd begun the day depressed, partly struggling with the relevance of Jesus. Now I was overwhelmed by the irony of my unbelief. Jesus had been sitting in our waiting room, right in front of me, as obvious as the daylight. I had walked by him all day. I had wondered if Jesus was around, and he had been silently waiting all day, saying nothing. It was a stunning display of patience.

Cynicism looks in the wrong direction. It looks for the cracks in Christianity instead of looking for the presence of Jesus. It is an orientation of the heart. The sixth cure for cynicism, then, is this: Develop an eye for Jesus.

I knew from my study of the Gospels where to look for Jesus. For the most part, his earthly life was hidden, like a seed in the field. If you were to look at a photo album of his life, you would not see him with the best and the brightest but with the low and the slow. The only photo of him with a famous person would be with Pilate at his trial, but then Jesus was in bad shape. The seed was beginning to die.

A principal source of cynicism comes from looking up at Christian leaders who have gotten Jesus' kingdom mixed up with their own. Ministry itself can create a mask of performance, the projection of success.

Everyone wants to be a winner. In contrast, Jesus never used his power to show off. He used his power for love. So he wasn't immediately noticeable. Humility makes you disappear, which is why we avoid it.

In order to see Jesus, I would have to look lower. I would have to look at people simply, as a child does. I began to ask myself, *Where did I see Jesus today?* I hunted for the difference between what others would normally be like and what they had become through the presence of Jesus. The presence of Jesus, the only truly authentic person who ever lived, would reveal itself in the restoration of authenticity in people. I'd see Christians whose inner and outer lives matched.

SPOTTING JESUS IN CLEVELAND

When we look for Jesus we can find him, even in seemingly mundane encounters, as I did one morning in Cleveland.

My friend Jim picked me up at six fifteen in the morning and drove me to a men's breakfast Bible study. The first thing he did was apologize for not praying for Kim the previous evening. He and I had talked about her over dinner and briefly prayed together. Rarely will someone apologize over such a seemingly small matter, or even admit something like that in the first place. His apology had the smell of Jesus about it.

At breakfast the men were reading a seventeenth-century Puritan book on a godly perspective of work. These men were taking seriously Jesus' exhortation to build their lives on the rock of obedience to his words. Not exactly edge-of-the-seat reading, but imagine if politicians or corporate executives caught in the latest scandal studied a book by Puritans on work!

When I went to return my rental car, the attendant greeted me cheerfully. When he saw my name on the receipt, he said, "You have a name from the Bible." He was partly witnessing, partly fishing for a fellow Christian, and partly just in love with the Bible. His cheerfulness and exuberant faith didn't reflect the seeming lowliness of his job. Once again, I saw the presence of Jesus.

While I was on the rental bus to the

terminal, Jill phoned. She was laughing so hard I had trouble hearing her. Earlier that week, the school bus manager had called us. He was concerned that Kim, who was still in high school, wasn't waiting for the bus to stop before she started crossing the street. As soon as the bus began slowing down, Kim would head across the busy street. Her autism made it difficult for her to wait.

So Jill used chalk to draw a box on our driveway and told Kim she had to stand in the box until the bus driver turned on the red light. When she called me that morning, Jill was standing in the pouring rain in the chalk box with Kim, laughing at the ridiculousness of her situation. It was the laughter of faith, rejoicing in tribulation because the tribulation was so funny. Again, the presence of Jesus.

Then my mom called while I was walking through the airport. She briefly described a situation where she'd been falsely accused and had realized she needed to unilaterally forgive without the possibility of reconciliation. No mention of the gory details, just a quiet reflection on her own heart.

Jesus was everywhere, transforming that mundane morning. With a little conscious reflection, it was easy to see the presence and the beauty of Jesus.

I found that the very thing we are afraid of—our brokenness—is the door to our Father's heart. A grace-saturated vision enables us to defeat cynicism and talk with our Father, restoring a childlike simplicity and wonder.

NOTES

1. C. S. Lewis, *The Screwtape Letters* (New York: HarperCollins, 2001), 171.
2. The French Enlightenment thinker Rousseau taught that children were born good but were corrupted by people. Not surprisingly, Rousseau had five children, all of whom he abandoned to an orphanage. Leo Damrosch, *Jean-Jacques Rousseau: Restless Genius* (New York: Houghton Mifflin, 2005), 202.
3. C. S. Lewis, *The Abolition of Man* (New York: Macmillan, 1978), 81.
4. Alan Jacobs, *The Narnian: The Life and Imagination of C.S. Lewis* (San Francisco: HarperSanFrancisco, 2005), 158.

ABOUT THE AUTHOR

Paul E. Miller is executive director of seeJesus, which includes A Praying Life Ministries. seeJesus is an organization that develops training seminars and interactive Bible studies for churches, small groups, and other ministries. He is the author of *A Praying Life*, *Love Walked Among Us*, and *The Person of Jesus Study*, an interactive study of the wonder of Jesus and his love. He and his team of staff seminar leaders travel widely and lead various seminars at churches, ministry staff offices, retreat centers, and international mission locations. Paul and his wife, Jill, have six children and live near Philadelphia.

For more information, visit seeJesus.net and APrayingLife.com or call (215) 721-3113. Follow Paul on Twitter: @_PaulEMiller.

Praise for *A Praying Life*

"What a refreshing book! If you're tired of religious prayer games and rote prayers that stop at the ceiling or if you have suspected that God was on vacation somewhere, this book will change your life. And if you're thinking about giving up on prayer, don't! At least not until you've read this book. When you have, you'll thank me for recommending it to you."

—STEVE BROWN, professor, Reformed Theological Seminary; teacher on the syndicated radio program *Key Life*

"Honest, realistic, mature, wise, deep. Warmly recommended."

—J. I. PACKER, professor, Regent College; author (with Carolyn Nystrom) of *Praying*

"Prayer, the concept and the practice, exposes our core doubts and desperation for God. Paul Miller captures the promise of prayer as a gift that connects us to the heart of the Father and as a path for transforming the world. Paul Miller's honest struggle with living a life full of prayer and his childlike delight in hearing the heart of God invite us to gratitude and call us to speak boldly to our God. This book will be like having the breath of God at your back. Let it lift you to new hope."

—DAN B. ALLENDER, PhD, president, Mars Hill Graduate School; author of *To Be Told* and *Leading with a Limp*

"*A Praying Life* is a deeply moving testimony to God's power in prayer. Paul Miller shares his life and biblical wisdom to instill in us, his readers, a 'heart that becomes a factory of prayer'—that is, a passion to speak to God honestly and in a way that will change our life and the lives of others for whom we pray."

—TREMPER LONGMAN III, PhD,
professor of Biblical Studies, Westmont College;
author of *Reading the Bible with Heart and Mind*

"If Jesus or Jesus' saving grace is just an abstraction to you, Paul Miller will be a great help in making his love a living reality to your heart."

—DR. TIM KELLER, senior pastor,
Redeemer Presbyterian Church, New York City;
author of the *New York Times* best seller *The Reason for God*

"Paul Miller refuses to separate the spiritual life from the rest of our daily living. In *A Praying Life*, he shows the difference that constant communication with Christ makes in the everyday experiences of life, especially the life of the family. Reading this book will help you make prayer a more important part of your own life story by integrating prayer into the daily routines of life."

—DR. PHILIP RYKEN, senior minister,
Tenth Presbyterian Church, Philadelphia, Pennsylvania;
author of *The Message of Salvation*

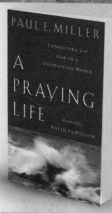